ETERNITY SMITH AND OTHER POEMS

JUANITA CASEY

ETERNITY SMITH
AND OTHER POEMS

THE DOLMEN PRESS

ETERNITY SMITH AND OTHER POEMS
is designed by Liam Miller
set in Palatino type by Koinonia Limited
and printed in Ireland by O'Brien Promotions Ltd,
for the publishers,

THE DOLMEN PRESS
Mountrath, Portlaoise, Ireland

The Dolmen Press receives financial assistance from
The Arts Council, An Comhairle Ealaion, Ireland.

First published 1985

British Library Cataloguing in Publication Data
    Casey, Juanita
       Eternity Smith and other poems.
       I. Title
       821'.914   PR6053.A8

ISBN 0 85105 432 3 limited edition
ISBN 0 85105 431 5 pbk

CONTENTS

Fadó Fadó, amárach. . .

Yeats would have that Horseman
End the song.
When I die,
You will see no sidhe nor shade
Pass by,
But fearless,
bear the accolade
Of the stallion's eye.

WE GROW OLDER

Perhaps we long
Not so much for
Prufrock's indifferent mermaids
Upon his beach.
But for those tides
To wash away
The old, used thoughts
And flotsam from around our minds—
Rearing sentinel as single rocks
In the eddies of ourselves;
Leaving us
Thoughtless new thought, perfect,
Pristine. . .
Ourselves, sand, the dry, lisping limpets,
Each
Endlessly waiting for that rush
Of cool water
In some hushed
And halcyon bay.

SAILING TO BYZANTIUM

Under the single blackthorn
In a tumbled Jericho of walls
An old white horse is dying.
The thorn's black arthritic sinews
Talon across the bank's back,
Clawing at a harsh life
Beneath storms that flail and whistle
Over its haunted silhouette,
Stark as Nike.
A scholar of classics passed once
And told us: Children, look!
A winged Samothrace—
Carved by the wind out of hard air
And its own sharp-edged defiance—
We thought him daft.
We told him of Something Fearful
That happened there
Once upon a long time,
A curse was it, a murder,
Shunned by fairies—
People had forgotten now.
The old horse leans as though across
A low gate barring a new dimension;
Foursquare bones prop up his felted hide
Like poles stretching the slack corners
Of his slumped Bedouin frame,
Fissured camel lips
Bobble and rub at the green foam
Stringing the bared sprung octaves of his teeth—
The haggard coffin head jerks suddenly,
Ropy tendons hoisting up the wooden neck
Like the gaff on a Galway hooker,
Mane flying a last ensign.
The cabuchon eye, lustrous as morion,
Glows dim as a lantern candle-fogged,

Searching beyond life's horizons;
Small flutter of sound through
Guernica nostrils
Knuckering to some remembered pleasure or presence—
If ever there was one—
Hounds running on an imagined skyline,
Perhaps a child, hesitant,
Proffering half a red apple,
Or the approach of the angel of death—
Whoever he leans to see, hopefully
Carries no halter.
Death's invisible fence splinters,
Falling, he becomes ditched and mired
In his last headlong struggle,
Pulled down along his sagged ridgepole spine
Like a stained and faded tent
In a third rate circus.
The hempen tail knocks, shivers, and whatever
Was trapped inside the big-top collapse
Has suffocated.
They come and pull him round for the lorry
By one lathe-hard leg
Parodying the up-turned kitchen table
We sailed on to
Byzantium.

VENUS

Darling! he said
I want you wild and free—
I didn't marry you for your
Domesticity;
That is for others, you fascinating
You!
My Goddess,
Wind-blown, hare-footed in the dew. . .
O never, never change
Nor bend to Time's black wand,
And leave O leave to others the
Duster in the hand. . .
Dear love,
Whom the wheeling stallion greets,
Around whose brow the flowering garland meets,
Who daisy-chains the white bull's fearful horns—
To whom the fiercest lion would gladly bring his thorns—
Upon this pedestal, my love, pray stand,
My dearest and fairest in all the seas and land;
And while, dear love, you're so
Good looking
We'll forget there ever was a thing called
Cooking. . .
Ten years-ten centuries pass,
Alas.
He has her by the throat.
Quote:
You must be a member of some blasted coven—
What's mouldering in the larder
What's burning in the oven!
Ashes to ashes—
God, now the Rayburn's bust,
And underneath my
Bed
There must be HUNDREDWEIGHTS of

Dust. . .
Or heavens-something
Dead. . ?
Now, all hinges literally,
Upon a curious tale. . .
Of when, lying in a field of hay—
Yes both, but
Separately, Coral,
How tiresome to be so
Moral—
She saw a little hairy man one day
Who loved her for herself,
And never pressed to see
Whether she was Housewife, Tart, Witch,
Goddess or Gilded Lily;
He grazed her stallions,
Kennelled all her hounds,
And with her, his delight in falconry
Knew no bounds.
When she said Dearest, I'm afraid
I cannot cook,
He said O yes I know—is
That a Jackdaw or a Rook?
While others called him simple,
Or a fool,
He dined with dogs and debris piled
Around his stool,
And islanded in mounting dust and
Dung
Merely blew his soggy porridge and conversed on
Jung.
Expecting nothing from the Goddess but
Herself,
No argument, recriminations, no blame or
Curse—
The Goddess went hard into
Reverse. . .

Now swept and polished even
Cobblestones,
And removed from behind the sofa spaghetti,
Fag-ends, knittings, one stiff left sock,
Cheese rinds, dead goldfish, paint-lids,
Half a marrow, a mummified hamster, two
Chinese pennies, a hibernating bat and
Bones,
And applying Brighto to every floor
And wall,
The Goddess cobwebbed, flailed and besomed
Kitchen, lounge and hall,
And taking orphaned kittens from the oven
Tried her hand
At steak Rossini, cuisses de grenouilles,
And chicken Maryland.
Back on her pedestal, you'll see her in
The Louvre.
With the strained expression of one who
Cannot prove
To be all things to all mens' love. . .
For, slamming shut the oven door—
Bent low—
Look dear, no hands!— they're in the
Escallopes de veau. . .
Time proves she never lost her charms,
Her smile, her poise, but merely both
Her arms.

KAWLO

Look, the Gypsies!
The Gypsies are coming!
You whisper it
Behind your regimented gates,
Looking up the blue road
Across your crimped, cramped hedges;
The east wind whipping
Grey, snow-fringed shawls of cloud
Over the common,
And the thin cold crouching
Like a black and sullen dog gnawing
At the bare bones of the heath.
Black blame to the Gypsies!
Black as the crow, black as we,
Ringed round the orange fire.
Steal and snap like the fox, you say. . .
Then, like the orange fox
We'll run our scorching brushes
Through the furze,
And set your Nomansland ablaze
With snapping cracking teeth of flames,
And whipping, black-maned smoke
Crow-winged black as we,
Dragoning into the black sky;
Old flash-tailed fox skittering by.
Where are they—we saw them—
You shout,
The Gypsies! The Gypsies started it!
And the common's raked ribs are gaunt
And spiked like the charred blackbird
On the butcher-bird's thorn,
Black as the thieving crow,
Black as we. . .
And on the blue road
Beneath the moon's knife-sliver

A child has dropped a rag
Of Indian pink and threaded silver
And you say,
Look, the Gypsies!
But the gypsies
Are gone.

WHAT ROUGH BEAST

This part of the garden
Was formal, enclosed;
Statues in niches
Among the high yew hedges
Engrossed in pondering
Their weighted checkmate.
Venuses smearing with lichen simpers,
Turbot-bellied Hercules pocked and pitted
By leprous marble flaking them into
A general paralysis of the inane;
A thyroid Laocöon,
Michelined with serpents,
With the curled papery fists
Of three dead spiders
Threaded into one corner of
A square shout.
And it was cold;
The sun yet to chin above the shaven maze,
The gardener snoring in a dream of chrysanthemums,
The child curled in the palm of the morning,
The toad returning on halting press-ups
To the hole beneath the rockery
To spend his day, caverned and introspective,
A small bulbous Buddha—
The jewel in his forehead the assassin's maggot—
In a shrine of moss.
The great marble pool a dark, sunken rectangle,
As though a coffin,
Burdened with a hundred leaden years
Had fallen through the original symmetrical slab
Leaving the bowing seasons
To fill up its mortuary with mourning leaves and
Fractions of rain;
Newts plimsolling its edges,
And carp turning and planing

Like the hand bags of drowning scullery maids
In perpetual dismay
At their own reflection
In their dark hall of mirrors.
Not yet the cuckoo,
Ringing green April with a circle of woodsong,
Not yet the gardener,
With his rhinoceros hands and tail of raffia,
Bent like a blameless horse
Down his boot ruled rows,
Not yet the child,
Tasting the humming silence
In the amber bowl of afternoon,
Fascination and pity curdling
With the wasps embalmed
In their jam-jar's false hostelry;
Not yet the toad,
That small warty kaliph, topaz of eye,
One foetal-wet hand tipping
The blue and white Japanese saucer
Left by the child—a bread and milk
Offering for her tiny goitered
Emperor in hiding.
Not yet the sun,
With one move taking the queen of the day
In the hot bronze game of the hours
On the sundial,
When it came up.
In silence.
The carbuncle of black water swelled, split,
Gaped like a green wound,
And it rested the great knobbed sceptre of its head
On the marble edge.
Hastening, mercurial ants tested, considered
And retreated from the spatter of drops
It scattered among the stone cracks,
And water lilies rocked their mariner bees

On leaves laid as though for frog feast
On a setting of rubbery platters,
Intestinal anchors stemming up from the slaughter house ooze
Where dragon nymphs lurk,
Masked for ambush.
Slowly, its head circled,
Like a massive, formless coagulation
Of flesh and cooling metal,
That had erupted lava-skinned and bubbling
From its casting in primeval furnaces,
Arapaima-scaled, hooded and escutcheoned,
Unseeing through its finned and weedy fringes,
Its frayed sockets blinded by Time's passover;
Then,
Quietly,
It sank again,
Dragging its fleshy filaments
Like a launching hull its slipway chains;
The lilies swelled and humped
On the black water
Like the scarlet frills on the neck
Of the keeling Miura,
And the ants emerged, hesitant
At the droplet edges as though
Upon a prospect of Lop Nor,
Before retracing the partners
Of their frenetic pavane.
And behind the hedges
The scent of roses strengthening
In the first sunlight.

CARENTAN

Wars, and the young men,
And the old men remembering
Wars;
And general and gypsy tumble and turn
As sharing the loam
Field Marshall Gregory Fitz-Uppingham Stones
(D'ye remember at Harrow
We called him the Worm. . .)
Has a heart still of flint,
And cold-shoulder bones
Little billeted Liberty Smith—
Now a pellet of mud
In the claw on the foot of a hare. . .
How brave we were,
Oh God of battle—
Not like the youth of today!
Bloody old fools,
To hear them prattle,
How brave we should be tomorrow. . .
And the swingled Percherons
Share and coulter, ridge and lay
Dead ploughmens' fingers
Like old pipestems of fragile clay,
And the yellow leaf
Blows down the furrow.

ETERNITY SMITH

ETERNITY SMITH

Up in the hills
We passed those Shepherds,
Their fire going well, and themselves
Sitting spun into silence
And their cloaks of frost.
Their flock warm behind them,
Capped with a cloud of breathing.
Their dogs ran out at ours,
Needling the sharp night with a quick stitch of teeth.
That was a cold night alright.
We had three asses,
I remember, and a Syrian stallion
Gone in his wind.
Two black mules, regular Gemini of disasters,
And a spavined camel which clicked his age
Like someone snapping fingers.
I remember it like yesterday.
It didn't matter to us
The town was jumping.
There's never any room for us, no need to write
No Gypsies Here,
We know it in a man's eyes.
We camped that night
In a bit of rough and rock behind the stable,
The camel grumbling like an Elder
As he went down
Like a tent when the ridge pole goes,
And folding his lips into
His perpetual disapproval, like someone
Putting their hands into sleeves for a sermon.
We'd soon a fire
From the bit of thorn he carried,
And some of his wool to start it.
The two mules

Knocked head, shaking their bells,
Blistered us with liquorice glances,
And scissored bits out of the stars with their ears.
The dogs, as usual,
Ran out when the man and woman passed,
And we called them in.
The man was old, and his feet
Twisted like camelthorn and as full of knobs
As a herm oak.
Seeing us, he pulled the stiff ass around
And came hesitantly back, bidding us
Good Evening.
The girl we thought his daughter.
She eased herself off the ass, ungainly
As a heavy fish pulled over gunwales,
And we saw
She was very near her time.
They'd tried a lodging, he said,
But had no luck, the place was full.
Mother, I remember
Went to the girl,
And the old man said my wife is very tired.
Well, it takes all sorts
To make a world.
Dad told them try the Inn, mush.
And the old man went, bending
Into the orange lit doorway,
Leaving the woman and their little dappled ass
By our fire.
Mother put down her best rug
And sat her down, and told her
They were welcome if her old man
Had no luck, and to have no fear
Should she start in the night.
As Ma was skilled with babies.
And we stared and got our faces slapped.
It's just like yesterday.

But the old mush came back,
And the innkeeper with him.
They could have the stable, Mam,
He said.
He was sorry he'd have to charge them,
But was sure they'd understand,
Things being what they were.
And mind we were off by tomorrow. . .
Mother said to be sure to come
If they were worried.
And the old man looked relieved,
With his white hair blowing about him like a pelican's feath-
ers.
We kids were asleep when
They called Mother.
The girl told her
She'd had pains on and off for a good two days,
But didn't want to worry
Her good man.
Mother laughed. His name was Joseph,
She said.
The poor old bugger was like
A dog at a feast,
Anxious to do anything, falling over himself
To help, scared out of his wits and as proud as punch
When the baby came.
We heard it cry, and stood at the door.
All of us,
Watching.
Mother was like all women then,
Fluffed out like a hen, suffering by proxy,
And aren't men beasts but never mind.
A lovely little boy, looking at the poor old mush
As though she thought
He couldn't have sired a glass of milk.
We offered to buy the ass
Cheap, but the old bloke said no,

He had a feeling
She would still be needed.
And one as gentle was hard to come by. . .
What's his name, Missus,
I said, and she smiled
And said Jesus.
He's not as black as we
I said, and she smiled
And smoothed my hair back out of my eyes.
And suddenly I wanted to give the baby
Something for luck, like we do.
How well I remember it.
And had nothing, only an old nail in one pocket,
Off a mule's shoe.
Take it Lady, I said, it's for luck.
And she looked at me with sweetness and sadness.
And then we moved on, us and the dogs
And the three asses, the Syrian entire,
And the racking camel,
But we chopped the nappy mules
For a dizzy young camel filly
With a curly colt.
And all the years later
When the gentlemen and soldiers came
And said You people are skilful
At plaiting and smithing,
And we made them that thorn collar
Thinking they wanted it
To put round the neck of a straying sheep
To stop her easing through gaps,
And made them the big nails
They asked for,
Beaten from copper over our fire,
And Barrabas a diddi
If ever I saw one. . .
All those years gone
And I gave him a nail.

And now these others. . .
Dordi, who would have thought it.
Dear Lord, who would have thought it.

The Mongol horseman
Cannot read, cannot write;
Ho, Jade Flower, he calls
To his snow-leopard horse,
And the ghost
Of General Ts'ao's lion-spotted stallion
Challenges the dust
Of the first Jade Flower
By the toppled red marble pillars. . .
The Mongol horseman
Rides down the summer wind,
Drifting grass seeds
Pepper the legs of the horse
Called Jade Flower—
Rare-coated as ermine.
The Mongol horseman
Cannot read, cannot write;
Blowing dust from his quilted sleeve,
Ho, Emperor of Hope, he calls
To the cuckoo. . .
Bending, he reads of himself
In the black agate bowl
Of the leopard stallion's eye,
And the wind, wetting the brush point
Of his horse's tail,
Writes in the grass
Of horses and emperors,
Generals and palaces,
And all the dynasties of thistledown.

HAIKAI

1

Child,
Holding out one hand,
See how the snowflakes
Lecture us.

2

Who has dreamed
The great salmon
Dreaming
Under the bridge—
Fisherman,
Cast no fly
And catch the
Dream.

3

What ghost passes
With a scent of lilacs
In midwinter,
With a child licking the frost
At the window?

4

After a spring shower
A dead swift on the path,
Beneath it a cross of
Dry dust. . .
Undisturbed, leave it to the rain's chance.

5

Dragging a violet shadow
A black mule wanders
Ringing a cracked bell.
No one is around the corner.

6

The caterpillar falls,
Crying
Life is a dewdrop.
People rush by, beneath
Umbrellas.

7

Why rage if the roof
Has holes?
Heaven is roof enough.

8

The winter coat of the old humped ass
Is chiming with icicles,
Yet they must cast
Great bronze bells to deafen Heaven.

9

Four crows on four posts
Across a field of mustard,
A chord for summoning foxes.

10

The learned
Philosopher
Comparing our lives
To the aimless snail's trail
Must not fear the gardener's boot. . .

DRAGONFLY

Anax Imperator.
One of the
Lower Orders
We call you, being the
Highest Animal
Of all.
I rescued you, drowning beneath
A crimson lily.
A pallid excalibur, half drawn
From a split and sodden
Scabbard.
And now,
You,
Anax Imperator,
One of the
Lower Orders,
Flashing your jewelled vizor,
Set your lance
At the sun,
While I,
With my higher intelligence,
Stand here, with feet
Of clay.

Anax Imperator,
Words, *words.*
Like these,
Poems and *Evolution.*
Of your giant
Warriors,
Jousting in the fern forests,
Before the thunder lizards.
Before us.
You were winged,
Even then,

Anax Imperator,
While we were
Spraddled
In the glazing, reptilion ooze;
Splayed, unthinking basilisks,
Shambling salamanders,
Slung on their wrinkled,
Sagging frames,
Like a dead tramp's bloated tent.
Words, words.
Poetry—
A Chinese puzzle,
Chambered and convoluted,
And crouched
Within its ivory labrynths,
Words
Like mazed Theseus,
Grope over the glistening walls
In the fissured, echoing caverns
Filigreed with stalactites
Of bone.
Evolution—
The lurcher at the heel
Of that oldest ghost,
Unreasonable, threadbare, hobo
Time.
Blind with prophesying
The past,
Forever remembering
The future,
Cracking his flint knuckles
In the whining wind,
And prizing our soundless translation
From the wordless jaws
Of stones.
Time, Evolution, Man,
Dog.

All words. . .
Now ginned and netted,
And brought warm to hand
By our new long-dog;
Here boy, here Sapiens.

Anax Imperator,
What does it
Matter,
Whether you are
Supposedly
A Less Order,
Or I am
Supposedly
The Higher,
As long as our children,
May pass in the sunlight
By a pool
Of crimson lilies;
Each rehearsal contained within
The glittering parable.
Yours,
Encased in the unended,
Scintillant flight
Of three hundred million summers,
Mine,
With the immortal wings
Of the mind, and feet
Of clay.

ZEN AND NOW

Reading Basho
Under fox-shared bracken,
Warblers distilling song
Out of early morning rain
And three swans pulsing
For a silver landfall;
That would please him—
Who'd have thought
Swans farted—
Plop!
The old pond and that famous frog. . .
Now we hear
It's a wrong translation.
Plop! an illusion.
Illustration: a buffalo,
Horned like a boomerang,
Carrying Grandpa
Rump-perched like a tinker;
In another, facing backward,
(All Desire Gone)
Like a kid on an obliging donkey.
A blank page—
'The Cow and Sage Quite Gone Out of Sight'. . .
Round the bend
Or through the gate,
The last water-buffalo
(With or without Sage),
The hundred Pythagorean oxen—
(The I-Ching: 'No Blame')
Or Mullingar heifer—
The cows of the world
Are the same;
Huffing strings of drooling effs,
Blatting flies with sinewy
Kelp-tails,

Pocketing the World
Through half-mast, megaphone ears,
And roundly gathering it in
With fish-bowl stares
Through gobstopper eyeballs;
'Quite out of Sight'?
Philosophy
Has forgotten the inevitable
Cowpat.

DEAD OWL

Tick tock
Owl clock
Time —mine—
Is time to be
Coming and
Doing and going
Boing
Gone. . .
Owl Time
Is a ratchet of briars,
Owl days wound rickety by the wren,
Disarticulation of the minutes
Into vole bones
And the ticking of dry ivy
In a whetstone grey easterly;
Owl winters, gobbets of woodmouse,
Rash at the fungus feast,
When frost sharp-hones the chimes
Ringing in air clean as an axe,
And snow zipped with a fox's short skelter
Into the old holly wood
Crouched canny with woodcocks.
As he fell, in the last long swoop
Into the dark,
He caught death in one claw, and
Clutched to his final kill,
Gripping in one wrinkled, razored gauntlet
The ultimate perfect nought,
A last wing beat
Shrugging him into a jacket of leaves
And on his time-piece face
All his owl hours stopped.
Time's legacies
A cast of owl bones, runes and prophecies
Thrown light as air,

With undeciphered shrew needles from
An old repast still shrill
With malediction;
Elfin bodkins to pierce the musty webs
In the three corners of a dream,
As though we'd entered
An old garden shed
And found instead,
Within a small whorl
Of contrary doorway winds,
Our minds,
Curled unblinking,
Sinuous as a sheltering fitch.
Come on! Come on. . .
But there has been
A magic, a design, a sign, and
Omens. . .
And I. . .
And I have seen
Time passing.
In time? is is time?
Am I in Time, or
For an owl hour
Left outside Time
Like a parcel at a cottage gate. . .
Didn't you hear!
No,
Time
Stopped
For
Me.
Mother! Father! and still
It's not what I want
To say.
I can say. . .
I can say I was
Between Times—

Nipped and
Dropped
Just past the end of a
Bat-eared chime
Swooped upon and stunned by
Cold-winged silence
Out of Time
And a never falling feather.

HOUSEMAID'S UNCONNECTED KNEE

God!
Cobwebs. . .
And, at the end
Ashes to ashes,
Dust to dust
They protest,
Not knowing neither is to be feared
Unless they fear
Themselves.
Then why should I,
With old besom or new broom
Demolish
God the spider,
The web of the universe,
And whack the
Dust
That is all of us
Into yet another arrangement. . .
Having become
Ourselves,
How pointless worrying about
Dust,
When by living and dying
We all settle
Somewhere else
All over
Again.

ALARUMS AND EXCURSIONS

The chance flash
Of vision and collision
Of eyeflash
Flaring across the mind
Like magnesium—
Fox, trotting pedantic,
Brush just so, nose unprepared
For our meeting in the green tree tunnel;
Eyeflash, and the cat flight
Light as a feather;
Sparrowhawk, grey-barred and frightening
As a Stuka
Wing-tipping low through the spinney
Straight for the no-kill
In a second's snapped-off decision;
Eyeflash, hissing past the face
With the yellow twin-bore stare
Of malevolence.
Or that alien chill
Rigid with the long poisoner's appraisal,
The fixed obsidian eye
Ring-set as a Borgia's jewel,
Of the braided viper—
As unexpected as an
Arab headband dropped
In such a place,
Before the re-nerving eye
Fastens the scaly necklace into the mind
Sliding among the olivine eggs
In the pheasant's nest;
Which of us finds
Eyeflash
As disturbing as that unease
Weaselling along the line

Of lingering cigarette smoke
In a hundred-acre, stretched and empty field.

AND THRIPS TO YOU TOO

Once upon a time
There was a gardener,
Who gardened,
And grew Wallflowers and Bellflowers,
Gillyflowers and silly flowers,
Kohl rabi, cold radish, Custodians
And broccolli,
Pellitory, Salsify, Suppository and Fustians,
Knapweed, Knotwood, Knitbone, Crimps,
And a rose called Monopoly;
Nasturtiums, Glaswegians, Geraniums,
Begonias, Harmoniums, Ribsache, and Cliggers,
Straight Alice, Wheeze-Not and Old Man's Suprise;
Borders and arbours of
Stand-up-Mother-Rundle, Lie-down-Pretty-Maiden,
Meddlers and Cravats, Bettinas and lettuces,
And in all sorts of crevices
He sprayed against
Nematodes, Willywogs, Merrytwats and Needlenodes,
Sitfasts and Buttonsnags, Pissymires and Mollylugs,
And the red-handed Haematodes
Which particularly relished
The rose called Monopoly.
Ah! Women! said the gardener,
Ah, *Women*. . . said the gardener,
Are the bane of the Garden—
(Henbane, Wolfsbane, Durdle-door and Goatsbladder)
They *will* pick all the
Wallflowers and Bellflowers, Gillyflowers and silly flowers
Kohl rabi cold radish Custodians and Broccolli
Pellitory Salsify Suppository and Fustians
Knapweed Knotwood Knitbone Crimps
Nasturtiums Glaswegians harmoniums Geraniums and
     Begonias
Ribsache and Cliggers Straight Alice and Wheeze-Not and

Old Man's Suprise—
Gasp—
Borders and arbours of Stand-up Mother-Rundle
Lie-down-Pretty-Maiden Meddlers and Cravats
Bettinas and lettuces and worst of all
DAMMIT
The rose called Monopoly.
Vexing I and Haggravating I and
Pussy-vanting around till
I Don't know me Uncle Izzie
From me Grandmother's Garters. . .
Howsomever moreover and worse
Said the gardener,
They don't allow I to spray
Nothing and naught.
Poor little things
Poor little things they say,
You're a wicked old man Mr. Bannister—
Poor little things. . .
See this cannister,
I say,
Well BUGGER OFF
While I spray the bleeding lot on the
Rose called Monopoly. . .
One day the gardener grew a
HUUUUUUUUUUUUUUUUUUUUUUUUUUUUUGE
Sunflower, mainly for
His parrot Jack.
Ha ha said Mr. Bannister, Who's a clever boy then,
You can pluck yourself, Jack,
for *I'm* alright.
Which was unfair as Jack was
Totally bald
And he never said a word in
Twenty years. Come Michaelmas.
And Mr. Bannister began to climb
Up the sunflower, in the general direction

Of the sun,
Laughing and climbing and
Laughing and climbing and climbing
And climbing and climbing and
Phew
Climbing and climbing and
Climbing and climbing and climbing and
STRUTH
Gasped Mr. Bannister as he passed
Kanchenjunga,
I wish I'd stayed down with me
Wallflowers and Bellflowers
Gillyflowers and silly flowers
Kohl rabi cold radish Custodians and broccolli
Pellitory Salsify Suppository and Fustians
Knapweed Knotwood Knitbone Crimps
Nasturtiums Glaswegians Geraniums harmoniums
Begonias Ribsache and Cliggers
Straight Alice Wheeze-Not and Old Man's Suprise
Me borders and arbours and Stand-up-Mother-Rundle
Lie-down-Pretty-Maiden Meddlers and Cravats
And lettuces and me dear old
Rose called Monopoly,
And spraying as he climbed.
To cut a long story
Shortstemmed,
After exactly
One hundred years, Mr. Bannister
And his by now empty
Canister, and by now also
Somewhat bowed, arrived through a
Pale pink cloud
Into a beautiful garden.
Pink thought Mr. Bannister
Like Women's legs thought Mr. Bannister,
Ahhhh *Women*. . . and still clinging to the
HUUUUUUUUUUUUUUUUUUUUUUUUUUUUUUUUGE

Sunflower
Came face to face with
God
Who was sweeping up sparrows.
Pssssssst! said Mr. Bannister, I say—
Can you get me off this thing er Archbishop is it...?
PESSSSSSSST!
Said God. (The First Gardener)
Let Us Spray.
And Did.
Poetic Justice said God, Though why
Poetic. . . You Can Never Find a
Rhyme for Justice.
Mustiness? Laxitive? How Annoying. . .
Mr. Tennyson—
Over Here a Moment, Please. . .
And the rose called Monopoly
Died out too.
Although one seedling,
Of a peculiar sort of
Blue,
Was crossed with
"Poetic Justice" and called after
Agnes Plodding,
Mr. Bannister's sister, who was
Really rather ugly.
But the parrot, (Agnes: 'that sodding Jack'),
Who was buried in the
Japanese onions, had
Loved her.
He was the only one who
Did. Ah, *Men*. . . said
God.

HELLO MUM!

FS524339 on all the trucks
Punching each other up the line,
87 something couldn't get it on those
Going down, to where
I remember,
One December
On the river bank
There was a double murder.
In both our gardens
The ubiquitous buddleia,
A path worn to remembrance
Of butterflies and hours;
Did anyone bring you flowers?
All those goose-grass minutes
Catching on the slow hours for you
Elbowing away your days,
And against a brick wall
A punctured ball.
Perhaps not, in your day.
But you can depend Mother, on the
Wet buddleia— *"Now, Colour Thought Violet. . ."*

And you, lumbered with me, in
Or outdoors.
Perhaps that's why I like
Dinosaurs.
Father Nameless (who
Lopped the crabapple,
Older than all of us?)
An idea, thin sown by strangers,
Fleshed with hydrangeas. . .
Me No-Name, (like a Red Indian,
You Minnehaha?) Hahahaha
Perhaps that's why I laugh a lot.
Another thing you can depend on—

They cut down the buddleia, Mother,
When they re-build.
And bees come and go, there are Marvels,
Rainbows, marriages, snow and hot dinners,
And losers or winners,
Winners and losers
Someone will plant roses.
Do you know, Mother, I was once very interested
In rhymes, prehistoric horses, lost dogs
And the Mariana trench.
Someone once said I looked French.

VOX HUMANA

We four meet
Suddenly.
Old ragged ewe pronking
To the high rocks, dropping
Bits of her blanket,
Fox a skipping mile
Up to the trees on the hill's crest
Clipped by the wind
Like a T'ang cob's mane,
And the stranger
From the car-door slam in the valley
Intent with murderous
Bonhomie. . .
Past the rabbit's bones.
Nice weather
And the back's atavistic bristle
Telling you he's now
The Watcher. . .
Past the rabbit bones.
To be like rabbit bones. . .
Not to be gathered or garnered,
Ironed-out, ironed-in or urned,
Wailed at, railed at or
Church-railinged,
And someone paid a small fortune for
Battering your name
Into a blockhead of granite;
Or that out-of-place
'Norwegian blue' marble with which
Superior Banks reflect your
No-account face.
To be like rabbit bones. . .
For the horse
Nudging the skull from his grazing,

For the fox
A-grin with the long shins,
For the bees
Combing among the clover-parted ribs
(Half a pollen-basket, here's no
Samson's lion),
And the soul gone
Light-footed as the hare. . .
And catching the hare
With a long-dog supple as water,
Delicate as an antelope—
Conservative friends protest
(Pinheads beneath the jeering tiercel)
Forgetting the same scream
Bred them.

MULLO

Rain's coming, I feel it
In my bones. . .
And though my ear is now
A snail shell in the grass,
I'll tell you where
The grey upland hare shall pass;
I am the fox where hedgerows meet,
And watch you on the road through
Curtaining meadowsweet,
And I'll show you where that
Old travelling potter Summer sat,
Hidden like a dormouse in a fist of hay,
Furled under ferns like a folded cat
In the primroses and marriage-petal May,
Fashioning a Lion Face-in-a-Sunflower plate,
And hanging it with a pin of cirrus
In a rent in the sky's tent.
Rain's coming, I feel it
In my bones. . .
And I'll tell you, child,
When comes the gold October lion,
Chasing the leaves and spiking them
With sharp claws of frost.
Let him sit beside you,
Beneath the yellow hedge,
And with a paw soft as a mushroom
He'll roll the last of the sun's oranges
Over that hill— no, child
They'll not be lost;
And before he's banished
By forges winter's iron, he
Will leave you
A crown of briony. . .
Rain's coming, I feel it
In my bones.

And child, loom—
Where old sack-shouldered Janus
And his hook
Have laid a plait of thorns—
Across that slid quilt of snow
I'll hem you a running stitch of
Weasels in a row. . .
Child, I am the ring fingered magpie,
I am the moon-horned heifer
With a pricked star in her eye,
And I am a bead of elderberry,
Coral spindleberry,
And I am the doeskin sloe;
For a tinsmith's spirit need not puzzle—
Need not have to know
What is his own alloy—
When over an autumn hedge he casts
A net of traveller's joy
And enmeshes only a dunnock's song. . .
Child, go along.
Rain's coming, I feel it
In my bones. . .
And still I cannot stay
In the one place;
For like smoke and hoarfrost and the quiet
Snows of death,
Life is a moment's drift
Of winter breath.
And there's not yet the man
In heaven or hell
Who can set a wire or spell
And boast he snared a ghost. . .

Rain's coming, I feel it
In my bones. . .

WE GROW OLDER

'I do not think that they will sing to me. . .' For me, Prufrock's bony cry is more terrible than 'Eli, Eli. . .' Christ died confirmed in hope, Prufrock lives on. And on. And on. Which is surely the greater horror.

VENUS

Story of my life, except I've never been wife to a house.

KAWLO

Black, Romany. To be 'kawlo' is a sign of true Gypsy blood. Kaliben, blackness; did Shakespeare know some Romany—he certainly mentions (Henry IV) the young prince being able to drink with tinkers 'in their own language'.

WHAT ROUGH BEAST

At around 5 years old this strange experience happened to me in one of the great English gardens, when left behind. Now, it returns as a smell—of dead gardeners hanging from rusty hooks in the earthy crypts of their vanished potting sheds, and shades of gamekeepers swinging among the dessicated stoats and magpies on their long ago gibbets. The 'assassin's maggot'—toads are often found with a hole in their heads, being eaten alive. Miura—a famous Spanish fighting bull breed.

WHAT ROUGH BEAST

Arapaima; a huge, primitive Amazonian fish, with scales beautifully and intricately incised and engraved.

CARENTAN

That coastal region of Normandy where so many lost their

lives. Swingle: the bar that keeps the traces apart and attaches them to ploughs or harrows or any implement without shafts.

ETERNITY SMITH
Gypsies on the Continent believe they were cursed to wander for ever for making the nails for the Crucifixion. Smith is a common Gypsy name (Petulengro in Romany; The Man of the Hoof). Eternity not so out of place when Christian names include Liberty, Defiance, Goliath, Freedom.

CHINESE CHARACTER FOR HORSE
General Ts'ao was a great painter of horses; among them the 'lion-spotted horse' of the Kuo family. The T'ang poet Tu Fu wrote of the priceless pink agate bowl presented to the General by the Emperor Hsuan-tsung for a particularly fine portrait. One horse, Jade Flower, 'they led one day to the red marble steps. . . and there was one Jade Flower standing on the dais, and another by the stairs, and they marvelled at each other' (as did Whistlejacket at his Stubbs portrait). The Emperor of Hope— the cuckoo. The ancient Emperor Wang lost his kingdom and dying, became a cuckoo, forever crying 'oh to go back again'. Finally, I only found out years later that the Chinese character for draught or wind is the same as that for grass. . . looking back while riding through long grass in early morning we are all joined by Time—especially those of us who are fascinated by the bizarre and colourful 'lion-spotted horse' down the centuries.

ZEN AND NOW
Bashô— perhaps the greatest of the Zen poets. Illustrations are a series '1O Stages of Spiritual Cowherding', depicting the Sage (Wisdom, Enlightenment) and the buffalo (THE WORLD: Desire, Emotions). Pythagoras sacrificed one hundred oxen to the Muses for granting him the under-

standing of his famous theorem. As the Taoist 'I-Ching' reiterates: No Blame.

DEAD OWL
This took over 50 years and three dead owls to perfect. I remember clearly this train of thought on finding the first owl when very small—I was an only child, perhaps if I'd had brothers and sisters I wouldn't have been so introspective; then again in my early thirties I found another, but nothing I then wrote was right. Recently I found my third, and this poem flew softly in without a word of alteration needed, I had written nothing for 10 years. The next morning an owl's feather was left on my door step.

AND THRIPS TO YOU TOO
Arrived just like that among the Webb's Wonderful.

HELLO MUM
On standing outside the house of my birth. To my unknown mother.

VOX HUMANA
Pronking: the impala's stiff-legged buckjump. 'Norwegian blue': for the purist, Laurvigite, much used on public buildings, with its glittering planes of light—'schiller'.

MULLO
Ghost, spirit, Romany. Some of the older Travellers used wonderful imagery when story telling or musing on Life's mysteries.